Walking to Bethlehem

An Advent Journey

25 imaginative devotions
for adults and children

by
Fay Rowland

Visit the author's website at www.fayrowland.co.uk

Typeset at Attic Studios, England
in Century Gothic and Harrington

Cover design © 2019 Elizabeth Thomas

Published by Thomas Salt Books

ISBN: 978-1-915150-02-8

Reviewers Say ...

"In the style of C. S. Lewis and Max Lucado, this devotional and practical Advent Calendar will help you ponder the promise and ask the questions. Fun, festive and frank, this is a journey you are invited along."

"Travel from BC to AD with seeing, hearing and doing to focus your mind on the road to Bethlehem. Fun and devotional, practical and creative."

"In a light-hearted way, Fay brings the emotions and feelings of the characters in the bible stories to life. In the 'To Think About' sections, she helps us to imagine what was going on through modern eyes."

"Take a turn off from the Motorway Madness that is the rush to Christmas."

"You have made the trek before, but not in this way. Travel at your own pace, ponder, reflect and create, as you rediscover the walk to Bethlehem."

"This book will help you to think about familiar stories differently and put some well-known Christmas music into context."

Acknowledgements

Many thanks to all the folks who have beta-tested these devotions, who have suggested songs or illustration designs, and who have found ~~tpyos~~ typos. Particular thanks to David, Fiona, Lilian, Nicola, Richard, Sharon and Steve. You're a galaxy of stars!

Grateful thanks also to all the good folks at Christ the King and St Botolph's with whom I have had the privilege of exploring God's world and word with families and children. God has greatly blessed me through you.

Thank you to the lovely community of scholars at Wesley House, Cambridge for insisting that even a mathematician can be a theologian, and for encouraging me to publish my work.

Special thanks to Steve D for the constructive criticism, editing suggestions, endless cups of tea and occasional stolen Kit-Kat.

And most of all, thank you to my children, Emily, Elizabeth and Eleanor, who have put up with a mum always going tappity-tap-tap on a computer, and with meals of chicken nuggets and chips because I was too busy to cook anything else. (I don't think they minded.) They are the ones who inspired the original set of readings and are still the reason I do most of what I do.

And Dwagony, of course.

Contents

Making Space

Life is busy. Life with kids is busier still. Life with kids just before Christmas is … phew!

So take some time from the frantic festivities. Wind down and come on a slow journey with Mary and Joseph. Savour the familiar texts and put yourself in the story of the world's most famous birthday.

Starting on December 1st, each day has a short reading and a prayer, plus an imaginative reflection. There are also suggestions for music and relaxing colouring.

There are resources at the back to mark the journey through Advent in creative ways.

Who Is This For?

Grown-ups and children, nativity ninjas, tiny tots and everyone between. There is something in these pages to help all of us engage with the story of Jesus' birth as if hearing it for the first time.

It is my prayer that all of us who use this book will discover new things about God and ourselves as we walk the road to Bethlehem, to meet the baby who changes everything.

Just For Kids?

Not at all! Grown-ups sometimes feel we have to put our creativity aside when we leave childhood, but God-given imagination can be a really useful tool for getting inside a Bible text.

The traditional Christmas readings can become blunted by familiarity, so it is good to let the story soak into your soul by reading slowly and thoughtfully. Using a different translation from your usual one can help as well.

Read the verses few times, and put yourself right in the action. What was it like then? What were they thinking? Where am I in the scene? What would I have done?

Come with me on the journey, whether this is your first time or your fiftieth.

How To Use This Book

Step 1 – Relax.

This is not about 'doing' everything. There's quite enough of that in the run-up to Christmas. This book is about 'being', about finding space, not adding more stuff to your long list of stuff.

Step 2 – Read.

The Bible passages are short and easy to read, so young children will be able to join in. Having short readings gives us time to savour every part of the familiar story, and helps us to take in some of the detail that we might otherwise skim over.

Step 3 – Choose.

Choose the sections that suit you. Perhaps you will think about the question in the car, or use the prayer during your lunch break. Perhaps you will have a labyrinth by your Christmas tree and move Mary and Joseph every day, or make the readings into paper chains to hang around the room.

What Can I Choose?

There are devotions for each day of December up to and including Christmas Day.

Each devotion follows the same format. Read The Bible Bit first, then choose from the optional sections:

The Bible Bit

A verse or two from the Christmas story as told by Matthew and Luke, with linked texts from Isaiah and John. Readings are from the New Century Version, an easy-to-read translation suitable for all ages and traditions.

Stable Scene

Add a character to your Nativity display so that the scene builds up day by day. Follow the wise men on their long journey, and see who arrives overnight on Christmas Eve.

In The Action

Imaginative musings on the passage, putting us right in the scene. Some are a little quirky, some more reflective. Take a few minutes with a cup of tea and a biscuit, and let the wonder of the story soak in.

To Think About

A question to help us consider our response to the text - challenging enough to engage teens and adults, yet accessible for younger children too. There are no 'right' answers. These are discussion starters, not tests of knowledge.

Responding

A short prayer in simple language. Easy for children to read, but addressing real issues that face us all. Suitable for personal or family prayers, or prayers from the front in schools or churches.

You could try writing your own prayers too. Putting words down on paper can be a great way to sort out our thoughts.

Listening

A varied selection of Christmas music to accompany your devotions. Some familiar, some less so.

Illustration

Colouring is not only for kids! Put on some music and grab your watercolours or pencils, then take a few minutes to think about the story for the day while you colour the illustration. I find it's a useful way to slow my busy mind.

You can photocopy the illustrations so that everyone can have a sheet. There are spare designs blank versions if you want to make your own patterns.

Counting Down to Christmas

This book started life as a way of marking Advent with my young children. Normal Advent calendars are great for counting the days, but I wanted my family to have something more meaningful than chocolate snowmen and elf hats. So I made mini books for my daughters, each containing one of these readings, and we still hang one on our Christmas tree each day.

Here are five ways to use this book during the long wait for Christmas:

Devotions

The next fifty pages have the daily devotions. You can use them alone or with any of the additional resources at the back of the book.

Scrolls

Use the photocopiable resources at the end of the book to make paper scrolls, then hang them on your Christmas tree each day. It's a fun craft as well as a stylish decoration.

Paper Chains

You can also use the strips to make a paper chain. It is decorative and works as a countdown calendar too – a visual reminder of the time left until the big day.

Posada Road

A great way to depict the journey to Bethlehem is with an actual journey! There are instructions at the back for how to make a mini road. You can put numbers along it to keep track of the days, and move Mary and Joseph towards Bethlehem each day.

Advent Labyrinth

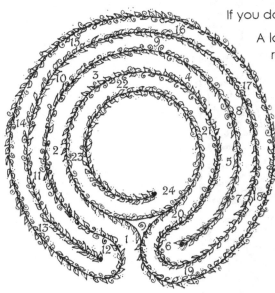

If you don't have room for a road, why not try a labyrinth?

A labyrinth is a winding path that leads to the centre, a road folded into a smaller area.

Mary and Joseph can move through the labyrinth, pausing at the numbered stops each day.

Young children can easily join in with this activity, following the numbers with the days.

There are instructions at the end of this book for making a large labyrinth.

Alternatively, you can print one of the designs onto paper and colour a section of the path each day.

Day 1 – An Eternal Plan

The Bible Bit

Luke 1:26-27

God sent the angel Gabriel to Nazareth, a town in Galilee, to a virgin. She was engaged to marry a man named Joseph from the family of David. Her name was Mary.

Stable Scene

Add Gabriel (angel).

In The Action

I wonder what excitement there was in heaven. It was time to put God's eternal rescue plan into action! I can imagine Gabriel stepping to the front of the crowd of angels.

"This is it guys." he says, "Today is the start of the biggest rescue in history."

"What do you mean?" ask the other angels, jostling to see.

"You remember God's plan to finally get rid of evil, destroy the power of death and rip down the curtain between him and humans? It starts today!"

The other angels are buzzing with enthusiasm. "Brilliant!" "I'll get my sword." "Can't wait to get into battle!"

"Stop, stop," says Gabriel, pulling back one particularly keen junior angel. "It's not going to be a battle. Well, not that kind of battle anyway. And it's only me going."

"You see, there's this teenager I have to visit. Her name is Mary."

To Think About

Why did God choose Mary, do you think?

Responding

Dear God,

thank you for your wonderful rescue plan.
You knew that we humans would go wrong and get lost,
and you planned to rescue us even before we knew we needed it.
Thank you for Jesus.

Amen

Listening

Rescuer (Rend Collective)
The Angel Gabriel from Heaven Came

Day 2 – A Strange Greeting

The Bible Bit

Luke 1:28-29

The angel came to her and said, "Greetings! The Lord has blessed you and is with you."
But Mary was very startled by what the angel said and wondered what this greeting might mean.

Stable Scene

Place Balthazar (wise man) far off.

In The Action

Imagine the scene: You are sitting at home, minding your own business, when there's a knock at the door. You put down your coffee / book / phone to see who it is.

And your jaw hits the floor.

There's a brass band outside your house. And a huge crowd of people clapping. And a film crew. There's a helicopter circling overhead, pom-pommed cheerleaders over to one side, and someone has let off a confetti canon. And you're stood there in your slippers.

A guy with a microphone leaps forward. "Greetings, you who are highly favoured! The Lord is with you," he says, stuffing the mic in front of your face. Nothing comes out of your mouth.

"What kind of greeting is this?" you wonder, feeling an idiot as your gormless expression is beamed live across the internet.

I wonder how Mary felt.

To Think About

What would you have said to the angel?

Responding

Dear God,

thank you that you are a God who likes to talk.
Sometimes it's very easy to know what you are saying, like Mary hearing the angel.
Most of the time it's not so easy.
Help me to recognise your voice when you speak to me.

Amen.

Listening

Hail, Holy Queen (Sister Act)
Hail Mary Full of Grace (15th century carol)

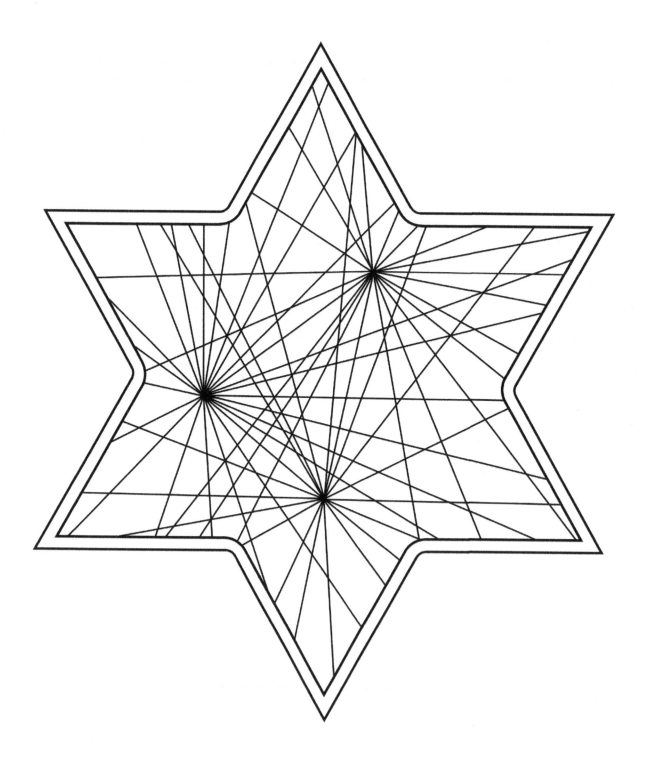

Day 3 – Do Not Be Afraid

The Bible Bit

Luke 1:30-31

The angel said to her, "Don't be afraid, Mary; God has shown you his grace. Listen! You will become pregnant and give birth to a son, and you will name him Jesus."

Stable Scene

Place Melchior (wise man) far off.

In The Action

What do you think about when someone mentions angels? Cute little blonde girls in white dresses and tinsel? Chubby babies with tiny wings and age-inappropriate archery sets?

Angels in the Bible are nothing like that. They are messengers, so think of a postman. They're also soldiers, so give your postman some armour and a sword, or maybe put him in a tank or jet plane.

And most people are pretty scared when they meet an angel. That's why the first thing angels say is usually, "Do not be afraid." They're a bit gob-smacking!

So take your soldier-postman and add the most famous person you can think of (who you'd never dare talk to) plus a bit of that really hard test that you're dreading. Add a smidgen of hungry lion, and I think you about have an angel.

Not so cute now, eh?

To Think About

What do you think an angel might say to you?

Responding

Dear God,

Thank you that you know when I am afraid,
and that you promise to always be with me.
Help me to remember this,
even when I think I am alone.

Amen.

Listening

Mary's Boy Child / O my Lord (Boney M)
It Came Upon the Midnight Clear

Day 4 – The Promise

The Bible Bit

Luke 1:32-33

"He will be great and will be called the Son of the Most High. The Lord God will give him the throne of King David, his ancestor. He will rule over the people of Jacob forever, and his kingdom will never end."

Stable Scene

Place Gaspar (wise man) far off.

In The Action

I often have no idea what my children are talking about. I expect they feel the same about me. My eldest daughter is musical, and her talk of 'A-flat demented' goes right over my head. However, we both like maths jokes. (Why is the horizontal axis called X? Because it is *a-cross*!) In maths, we each understand what the other is saying.

I wonder how long it was before Mary understood what the angel was saying.

"You're going to have a baby," – Duh, I'm about to get married.
"He will be great," – I'm sure he'll be adorable.
"And will be called the Son of the Most High." – Ummm, son of Joseph, surely?
"The Lord God will give him the throne ..." – hang on, throne? Why would a carpenter's son have a throne?
"... of his father David," – who's David?!? Oh, wait a minute, you don't mean ...?
"and his kingdom will never end" – Oh, I see. *That* king. The one we've been waiting for.
The Promised One. Wow.

To Think About

What helps you to understand?

Responding

Dear God,

you always keep your promises, but sometimes we have to wait.
Help us to remember that you always do what you say,
even when we cannot see it yet.

Amen.

Listening

The Promise (Michael Card)
Come, Thou Long-Expected Jesus

Day 5 – But ... How?

The Bible Bit

Luke 1:34-35

Mary said to the angel, "How will this happen since I am a virgin?" The angel said to Mary, "The Holy Spirit will come upon you, and the power of the Most High will cover you. For this reason the baby will be holy and will be called the Son of God."

Stable Scene

Add stable.

In The Action

A bit earlier in this chapter, there is another 'send an angel to announce a baby' thing, but it hadn't gone so smoothly that time.

Zechariah and Elizabeth had been praying for a child for years, but when an angel popped by and told Zechariah that his wife would soon have a son, Zechariah didn't believe him. "Will this really happen?" he asked. "How do I know you are telling the truth?"

I can imagine Gabriel drawing himself up to his full (probably rather impressive) height, rustling his feathers and giving Zechariah a narrow-eyed stare. "I am Gabriel", he says, "I stand in God's presence. And you doubt my word?"

Mary's question is very different. She knows that God will do what he says. She just wonders how.

To Think About

What question would you like to ask God?

Responding

Dear God,

I have questions. A lot of questions.
Some of them I have not formed in my head yet.
Thank you that it's OK to ask you questions
and it's OK to not know all the answers.

Amen.

Listening

Holy Child (Vineyard)
Infant Holy, Infant Lowly

Day 6 – According To Your Word

The Bible Bit

Luke 1:38

**Mary said, "I am the servant of the Lord. Let this happen to me as you say!"
Then the angel went away.**

Stable Scene

Add sheep.

In The Action

Now here's a thought. What if Mary had said no?

"No, I can't be pregnant. My parents would be so angry."
"No, I can't do that to Joseph. He'd refuse to marry me, and I'd be disgraced for the rest of my life."
"No, it's too much to ask. I can't do it."

It would not have been unreasonable. Saying yes could have ruined Mary's life. It nearly did. 'No' would have been the sensible choice, the safe choice, the easy choice.

But Mary didn't say no. Mind you, she didn't say yippee either.

This was no easy task that God had put before her. It was not going to be a walk in the park. But she and her people had been waiting for this rescue for so long. How could she refuse?

Maybe God knew that she would say yes, and that's why he asked her.

To Think About

What do you think would have happened if Mary had said no?

Responding

Dear God,
thank you for Mary's courage and strength.
May we have her bravery and confidence to trust you,
when you ask us to do difficult things.

Amen.

Listening

Mary, did you know?
Let it Be to Me According to Your Word

Day 7 – The Song of Mary

The Bible Bit

Luke 1:46-49

**Then Mary said, "My soul praises the Lord; my heart rejoices in God my Saviour.
From now on, all people will say that I am blessed, because the Powerful One has done great things for me. His name is holy."**

Stable Scene

Add star.

In The Action

Mary goes to visit her cousin Elizabeth, who is heavily pregnant, and stays for three months to help with the birth. I wonder if Mary has heard the story of Elizabeth's husband, Zechariah, and his encounter with the angel. Perhaps that's why she went to visit.

I wonder also if Mary has told Elizabeth that she'd had an angel visitor too and that she, Mary, was also expecting a baby. Or perhaps Mary is keeping that to herself for the moment.

But as soon as Mary walks through the door, her secret is out. "Blessed are you among women, and blessed is the child you will bear!" Hugs all around and probably quite a few joyful tears.

Elizabeth's delight is catching. All of Mary's pent-up emotion comes flooding out and she bursts into one of the most famous songs in the Bible.

To Think About

What would your song be?

Responding

Dear God,

you have lifted up the humble
and filled the hungry with good things.
You have done great things for me,
and you show your mercy for ever and ever.
Holy is your name!

Amen.

Listening

My Soul Proclaims the Greatness of the Lord (John-Michael Talbot)
Magnificat Anima Mea Dominum (Taizé)

Day 8 – Back to Reality

The Bible Bit

Matthew 1:18

Mary was engaged to marry Joseph, but before they married, she learned she was pregnant by the power of the Holy Spirit.

Stable Scene

Add sheep.

In The Action

Mary's song is a high point of the Christmas story, and I love the glorious free expression of her joy. But now it all comes down to earth with a crash.

Joseph. He has to be told.

Did Mary tell him, or someone else? Perhaps the news got back from Elizabeth and Zechariah's. Or maybe Joseph spotted Mary's growing bump and worked it out for himself.

No matter how it happened, there is some serious talking to be done. How is Mary going to explain the baby? Does she tell Joseph about the angel? Will Joseph believe her?

I can imagine a knot of anxiety in the pit of Mary's stomach as she sits with Joseph. Her heart is breaking as well as his as she sees the disappointment on his face.

"How could she?" he is thinking. "I trusted her."
"Please God, tell him it's OK."

To Think About

What do you think Mary said to Joseph?

Responding

Dear God,
Sometimes we hurt the people we love.
It feels horrible and it's hard to know how to make things better.
Please heal the wounds that we have caused
and the wounds in us.
Amen.

Listening

Somewhere In Your Silent Night (Casting Crowns)
Breath of Heaven (Amy Grant)

Day 9 – Disaster?

The Bible Bit

Matthew 1:19

Because Mary's husband, Joseph, was a good man, he did not want to disgrace her in public, so he planned to divorce her secretly.

Stable Scene

Move wise men closer.

In The Action

What a dreadful decision. Joseph is a good man and wants to do right according to Jewish law. But he also loves Mary and wants to do right by her.

If he marries Mary, people will think badly of him. No matter, he'll stand by her despite the nasty looks. But what would God think? That's the big question. Joseph can handle public humiliation, but to have God frowning on the marriage would be unbearable. No. He cannot marry her.

But then what? Public disgrace for the girl he loves? She'd be thrown out of her father's house, and you can be sure that no-one else would marry her. What then? Life as a beggar? He can't let that happen.

With a heavy heart, Joseph chooses the best of a bad set of options. If he quietly cancels the wedding, perhaps no-one will notice. And Mary? He'll keep an eye on her, and make sure that she and the baby are OK.

To Think About

What would you have done?

Responding

Dear God,

Sometimes it is easy to choose between what is good and what is bad.
But other times there is only a choice between bad and bad.
Please look after people who are in difficult situations
and help them to find solutions.

Amen.

Listening

Baba Yetu / Our Father
Millennium Prayer (Cliff Richard)

Day 10 – Son of David

The Bible Bit

Matthew 1:20

An angel of the Lord came to Joseph in a dream. The angel said, "Joseph, descendant of David, don't be afraid to take Mary as your wife, because the baby in her is from the Holy Spirit."

Stable Scene

Add animal.

In The Action

Have you noticed how many surnames end in 'son'? The angel who visited Joseph in a dream called him Joseph Davidson. But earlier in this chapter, he was Joseph Jacobson. Did the angel visit the wrong Joseph?

Or was the angel was looking more at the future than the past?

Sure, Joseph's father was Jacob. He was probably a carpenter too, and his father before him and his father before him. And that would be the plan for Joseph's eldest son as well.

But Joseph was also descended from King David, Israel's shepherd king. And that was more the heritage and career path that God had in mind for his son.

Note - There is a different family list in Luke. The word translated 'son' also means son-in-law, so one list could be Mary's family and the other Joseph's.

To Think About

How much do you think that the past determines your future?

Responding

Dear God,
it is amazing that you adopt us into your family
and tell us to call you Our Father.
You are the perfect Father.
Thank you that you call us your children.

Amen.

Listening

Once in Royal David's City
Baby Boy (For King and Country)

Day 11 – What's in a Name?

The Bible Bit

Matthew 1:21

The angel said, "She will give birth to a son, and you will name him Jesus, because he will save his people from their sins."

Stable Scene

Add animal.

In The Action

Some names have meanings, but you never know if a name will suit. Call a baby Rufus (meaning 'red') and there's no guarantee that he'll end up with red hair. Abigail ('my father's joy') could be a right grump.

Joseph's name means 'he will add'. I suppose being good at maths would be useful for a carpenter.

So what about Jesus, the name that the angel told Joseph to call his son. Did it fit?

Jesus is our version of 'Yeshua' and it is the same name as Joshua. Both mean 'The Lord saves', so I guess he lives up to his name pretty well!

To Think About

What name do you think God would give to you?

Responding

Dear God,

You know me inside and out.
You see my heart and my dreams.
You have written my name on the palm of your hand.
Thank you that you know me.

Amen.

Listening

Joseph Dearest
Joy has Dawned

Day 12 – God With Us

The Bible Bit

Matthew 1:22-23

All this happened to bring about what the Lord had said through the prophet: "The virgin will be pregnant. She will have a son, and they will name him Immanuel," which means "God is with us."

Stable Scene

Add animal.

In The Action

Choosing baby names can be tricky. Listen to these new parents:
"I've always liked Teresa."
"Our surname's Green, think about it."
"Teresa Gre ... Oh, good point. I guess Emerald is out as well."

So imagine the scene in the heavenly coffee bar when the Trinity were discussing names.
"How about Immanuel?"
"I thought we'd decided on Jesus. Is Immanuel going to be a middle name?"
"More a nickname."
"What, along with Prince of Peace, Messiah and all that? How many names does a kid need?"
"Yeah, but this one's important. It means 'God with us'."
(Sideways glances across the table.) "What, actually *with*? Literally *with*?"
"Yup. Totally with. Right there in the chaos and confusion."
"You sure about this? It won't be easy."
"Nothing this important ever is."
"Good point. Jesus Immanuel it is."

To Think About

What must it have been like for God to become a human and live in our world?

Responding

Dear God,

thank you that you lived with us in the mess and muddle of our lives.
Thank you that you left the glory of heaven to be with us, so that we can be with you.

Amen.

Listening

O Come, O Come, Emmanuel
Like a Candle Flame (God is With Us, Alleluia)

Day 13 – Bad Timing

The Bible Bit

Luke 2:1, 4-5

Augustus Caesar sent an order that all people must list their names in a register. So Joseph left Nazareth and went to Bethlehem in Judea, known as the town of David. Joseph registered with Mary, to whom he was engaged and who was now pregnant.

Stable Scene

Add donkey.

In The Action

Joseph has just told Mary they have to travel to the other end of the country. Mary is heavily pregnant, so this could not have come at a worse time. I wonder what Mary prayed.

"Seriously God, what are you playing at? Why does this have to be now? You asked me to carry your child, and it's not been easy, but I said I'd do it. And now this? I'm as big as a whale, my feet are swelling up like balloons and I need to wee every five minutes. And now I've got to walk to Bethlehem! Could you possibly make life any harder, do you think?"

Does that sound a bit disrespectful? Check out Psalms. There's plenty of yelling at God there. Plenty of telling God that life is not fair. Plenty of "why does it have to be like this?"

It's OK to tell God when you are cross, even cross with God. He knows already, so we don't need to pretend everything's fine when it isn't. It's OK to be not OK.

To Think About

What do you think Joseph said to God?

Responding

Dear God,

Sometimes following you is easy.
Sometimes it is hard.
Help us to stick with you
though the rough times as well as the smooth,
the same as you stick with us.

Amen.

Listening

O Little Town of Bethlehem
Little Donkey

Day 14 – Is That It?

The Bible Bit

Luke 2:6-7

While they were in Bethlehem, the time came for Mary to have the baby, and she gave birth to her first son. Because there were no rooms left in the inn, she wrapped the baby with pieces of cloth and laid him in a feeding trough.

Stable Scene

Add manger.

In The Action

"I don't know what I else expected. He's a lovely baby, but ..."
"But what, Mary?"
"Well, after all the fuss with the angels and him being the world's saviour and so on, I suppose I thought he'd look ... I dunno ... different, somehow."
"Different? You mean you didn't expect him to look like a wrinkly prune?"
"Hey, show some respect. That's God's son you're talking about."
"My son too. Kinda. Is it OK if he calls me dad?"
"I'm sure that's fine. But ... but he's so small. So helpless. What if I drop him?"
"You won't drop him."
"What if he gets sick? What if he gets a cut from your saw, and it gets infected and he dies?"
"That won't happen. We'll be careful. Anyway, that's years in the future. He's only been born a few hours."
"But how can I protect him and make sure he never gets hurt?"
"I don't think you can, Mary."

To Think About

How can God be a helpless baby?

Responding

Dear God,

you are so great and powerful, yet you became a helpless baby.
You are so majestic and awesome, yet you became like one of us.
Thank you for coming to meet us.

Amen.

Listening

Away in a Manger
Silent Night

From Heaven You Came / The Servant King
For Unto Us a Child is Born (Messiah)

Day 15 – Hidden Glory

The Bible Bit

John 1:14

The Word became a human and lived among us. We saw his glory – the glory that belongs to the only Son of the Father – and he was full of grace and truth.

Stable Scene

Move wise men closer.

In The Action

Imagine the period of quiet after the stress and hassle of Jesus' birth. The mess has been cleared up. Mary's had a cup of tea and some toast. Someone has found a clean blanket for the baby.

No shepherds, angels or wise men have yet turned up. It's just Mary, Joseph and this new baby.

Is the baby sleeping? Crying? Feeding?

I wonder what he looks like. A big, chubby baby or small and slender? Does he have any hair?

What is Joseph doing? Perhaps he's using his handyman skills, making something useful. Perhaps Mary is shushing him so that she and the baby can sleep.

And what is Mary doing? I wonder what she thinks as she looks at this little bundle of humanity cradled in her arms. Of course, every new baby is beautiful, perfect, a miracle. But this one …

To Think About

Put yourself in the scene. What would you be doing?

Responding

Dear God,

You made your dwelling among us.
You came to live in our neighbourhood.
You made yourself like us,
so that we could see your glory.
That is amazing.

Amen.

Listening

Joseph's Song (Michael Card)
Light of the world (Here I am to Worship)
Noel (Chris Tomlin)

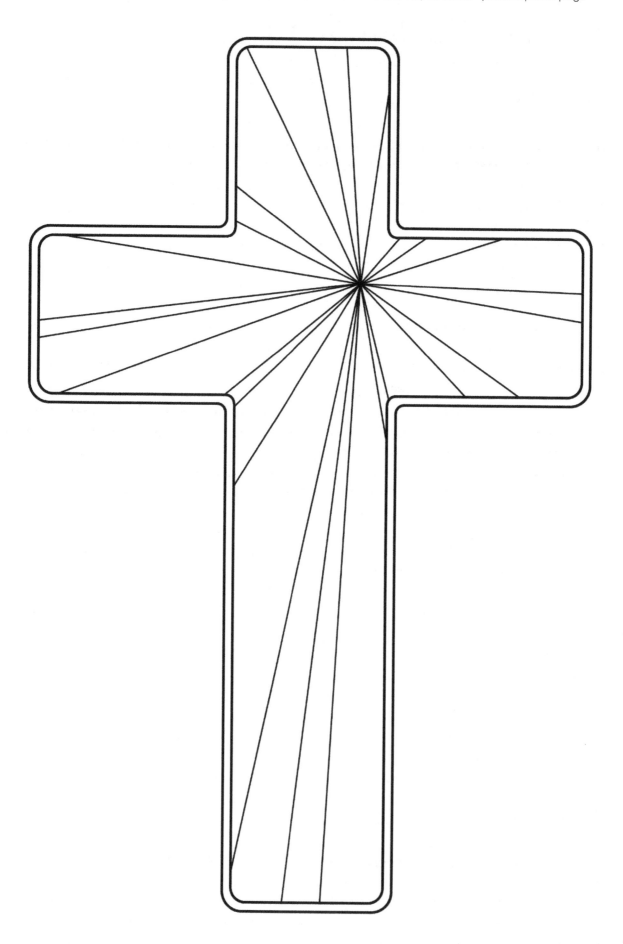

Day 16 – Awesome or Awful?

The Bible Bit

Luke 2:8-9

That night, some shepherds were in the fields nearby watching their sheep. Then an angel of the Lord stood before them. The glory of the Lord was shining around them, and they became very frightened.

Stable Scene

Add Michael (angel).

In The Action

When we think about shepherds and angels today, it's quite a nice image – boys wearing tea-towels and holding toy sheep, girls dressed in white with tinsel in their hair.

It wasn't like that, the first Christmas. These shepherds were the outdoors type. They slept in the fields at night. They fought off animals that attacked their sheep. They probably wore big boots and camo trousers.

These weren't little boys in dressing gowns. These were tough men. They had faced down wolves. And these tough guys were terrified of an angel?

We can be sure that this angel looked nothing like a cutesy 6-year-old with tinsel in her plaits.

Awesome? Yes, and Awful!

To Think About

What do you think the angel looked like?

Responding

Dear God,

These men fell to the ground in fear
at the sight of one angel.
But you promise that we will see you face-to-face,
and know you as you know us.
Wow!

Amen.

Listening

While Shepherds Watched Their Flocks by Night
The First Nowell

Day 17 – Good News

The Bible Bit

Luke 2:10-11

The angel said to them, "Do not be afraid. I am bringing you good news that will be a great joy to all the people. Today your Saviour was born in the town of David. He is Christ, the Lord."

Stable Scene

Add Uriel (angel).

In The Action

Final score, 3-0. Good news or bad? Depends on whether you're Rangers or Celtic.

Everyone likes good news, but good news for one person might be bad news for another. Rain – great for gardeners, not so great for holidaymakers. Hot dogs for tea – good news for the kids, not so good for the dog. Oh, wait …

But here, the angels bring a message that is good news for *everyone* in the world. Everyone. This is not simply good news. This is Good News, with capital letters!

This is something bigger than getting rid of the Roman invaders. This is something better than getting your dream job or marrying the one you love. This is something more lasting than winning a bazillion pounds. This is the best news that ever has been, that ever will be, that ever *could* be.

This is real, proper, eternal Good News.

I wonder what it could be.

To Think About

What is it like to hear Good News?

Responding

Dear God,
Thank you that you have Good News
for all people, in all places, at all times.
Help me to be part of your Good News
to everyone around me.

Amen.

Listening

Joy to The World
Come Love Carolling

Day 18 – Perfect in Weakness

The Bible Bit

Luke 2:12

The angel said, "This is how you will know him:
You will find a baby wrapped in pieces of cloth and lying in a feeding box."

Stable Scene

Add Zadkiel (angel).

In The Action

Joseph was a carpenter. I bet he'd made a lovely little cot for Jesus, back home. I bet Mary had a load of blankets ready, and a cute little hat that Grandma had knitted. I expect they'd asked neighbours to come round and help with the birth, and someone was bringing them a stew for afterwards.

All those great plans, and what did they end up with? A manger. An animal's feed box. And a borrowed one at that. Could the baby not have come a week or two later, when they'd got back home? When they were ready?

But perhaps that's part of the story.

The Bible is full of people who didn't feel ready – Moses, Isaiah, Jonah – but God called them anyway. Mary and Joseph didn't have all their baby stuff. But the baby came anyway.

God does not mind if we don't feel ready. The Bible tells us that God's power is made perfect in weakness. I wonder what that means for me.

To Think About

What are your plans? Do you think they are the same as God's?

Responding

Dear God,

It feels safe to prepare and to have things ready,
but sometimes our own plans get in the way of yours.
Help us to hold lightly onto our ideas,
and to be ready to change what we think we are doing.

Amen.

Listening

Calypso Carol (See Him Lying on a Bed of Straw)
Gloria / Angels We Have Heard on High

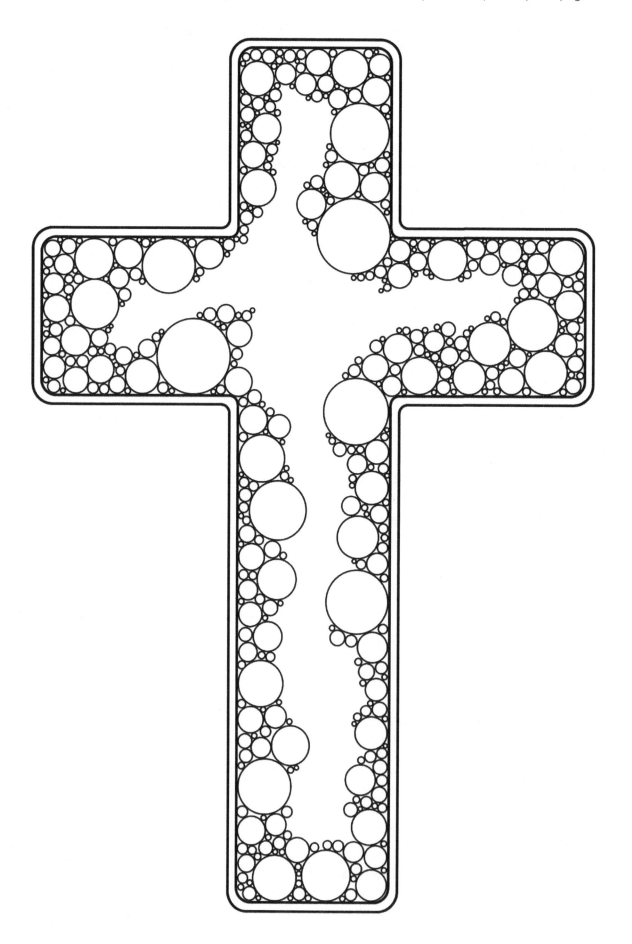

Day 19 – Turned up to Eleven!

The Bible Bit

Luke 2:13-14

Then a very large group of angels from heaven joined the first angel, praising God and saying: "Give glory to God in heaven, and on earth let there be peace among the people who please God."

Stable Scene

Add Raphael (angel).

In The Action

Sometimes God talks in a still, small voice, a sense of lasting peace, a feeling of wholeness and home. In the Old Testament, God spoke to the prophet Elijah in a gentle whisper.

Sometimes God shouts like a trumpet blast. God spoke to Moses like this through the burning bush, the plagues, and the fire and thunder from the mountain. Perhaps Moses wasn't very good at hearing God's small voice.

I wonder how many times I miss what God is saying to me because I'm not very good at hearing the small voice. I wonder how loud God has to shout to get over the din of my life. I think I need to spend more time in the quiet.

God spoke quietly to Mary. God spoke quietly to Joseph. But the shepherds got the fully heavenly choir with the volume turned up to eleven!

There was no way you could miss this message, and it was a message worth shouting about!

To Think About

How can we hear God's voice better?

Responding

Dear God,

Thank you that you speak to us in the quietness of sunrise.
Thank you that you speak to us in the power of storm.
Thank you that you speak to us in the beauty of birdsong.
Help us to hear your voice today.

Amen.

Listening

Hark the Herald Angels Sing
Glory, Let There Be Peace

Day 20 – Shepherd King

The Bible Bit

Matthew 2:5-6

The prophet wrote about this in the Scriptures: 'But you, Bethlehem, in the land of Judah, are not just an insignificant village in Judah. A ruler will come from you who will be like a shepherd for my people Israel.'

Stable Scene

Add Laban (shepherd).

In The Action

Kings and queens – what comes to mind? Crowns and robes? Huge banquets, with tables creaking under mountains of fancy food and a dozen knives and forks at every place?

I don't know about you, but I'd feel very out of place at a feast like that. I don't like wine, I'd forget to curtsey in the right places, and I'd probably try to use the fish knife to eat my soup.

No, I'd be much more comfortable downstairs with the servants. Perhaps a nice pie for dinner, with mash and gravy and as much tea as I can get down my neck. That's more like it!

But then – gasp – the Queen pops her head around the door. "Do you mind if I join you?" she asks, and slides into the chair between Jenny, the second under-housemaid, and Sebastian, a trainee gardener.

A Queen who scoffs pie and mash? Unheard of! A King who is like a shepherd? Nonsense!

To Think About

How would you feel if God invited you to join him at his banquet?

Responding

Dear God,

It is amazing that you, the ruler of the universe
can be bothered with ordinary people like me.
Thank you that you invite me to join your banquet,
and thank you that you won't mind if I use the wrong fork.

Amen.

Listening

The Lord is My Shepherd (Howard Goodall)
Do You Hear What I hear?

Day 21 – Talking and Thinking

The Bible Bit

Luke 2:16-17, 19

So the shepherds went quickly and found Mary and Joseph and the baby, who was lying in a feeding trough. When they had seen him, they told what the angels had said about this child. But Mary treasured these things and continued to think about them.

Stable Scene

Add Amos (shepherd).

In The Action

Have you seen the film *The Princess Diaries*? It's about Mia, a teenager who discovers that she is the heir to the throne of a tiny country. Mia keeps this a secret, telling only her closest friend.

I can understand. She needed time to get her head around the big change. Life would never be the same after this.

But the secret gets out and Mia's quiet life becomes a media circus. For the newspapers and TV crews, this is exciting news. They can't wait to tell the world. For Mia, it's a bit more complicated.

It's the same with Mary and the shepherds. The shepherds told everyone, "This baby is our long-awaited saviour!" Mary sat quietly and wondered what it all meant.

I can understand. She needed time to get her head around the big change. Life would never be the same after this.

To Think About

Would you have told everyone, or thought for a while? Or a bit of both?

Responding

Dear God,

Help us to be like the shepherds,
who were so excited at your Good News that they told everyone.
And help us to be like Mary,
who thought deeply about what the Good News meant for her.

Amen.

Listening

In the Bleak Midwinter
When a Child is Born

Day 22 – All May Come

The Bible Bit

Matthew 2:1-2

When Jesus was born, some wise men from the east came to Jerusalem. They asked, "Where is the baby who was born to be the king of the Jews? We saw his star in the east and have come to worship him."

Stable Scene

Move wise men closer.

In The Action

I wonder what the wise men were thinking when they set out on their journey. They probably travelled from Persia, and that's a long journey to see a baby who is someone else's king.

Would they even be welcome when they got there? Persians and Jews didn't exactly have a happy history, so they might be turned away at the door. Perhaps the king of the Jews would refuse to see them. They were outsiders, after all. The whole journey might be a waste of time.

But time after time in the story of God's people we hear about strangers from other lands coming to worship God. Some of them are mentioned in Jesus' family tree. And when Jesus grew up, he would shock the religious leaders by welcoming outsiders, by eating with outcasts, by forgiving the unforgivable.

Three strangers come to worship. Perhaps they are not the 'right' kind of people. Perhaps they don't fit in. But all may come.

To Think About

Who might not fit in today?

Responding

Dear God,

thank you that you welcome all kinds of people into your family.
Thank you that you welcome me, with all my broken bits and weirdness.
Help me to spread your welcome to others, with all their broken bits and weirdness.

Amen.

Listening

As with Gladness Men of Old
What Star is This?

Day 23 – Star of Wonder

The Bible Bit

Matthew 2:8-10

Herod sent the wise men to Bethlehem. The star that they had seen in the east went before them until it stopped above the place where the child was. When the wise men saw the star, they were filled with joy.

Stable Scene

Add wise men.

In The Action

The wise men were what we might call scientists today. And although stars don't actually tell us where people are born, or what they're like, God used the understanding of the day to guide these astronomers to the right place.

They were filled with joy at seeing the star, but were they filled with joy at where it led them?

I wonder what they thought when they found their journey ended here. *Is this it? Surely this can't be right.*

I wonder what they thought when they got their lovely robes dirty from the stable floor. *Where's the king? Where are the servants?*

I wonder what they thought when they met the obviously not-royal baby. *Seriously? Did we come all the way here for this?*

Sometimes it's hard to see God when he looks like a human.

To Think About

Who can you see God in today?

Responding

Dear God,

you call us to shine your light and to reflect your glory.
Help me to glow with your goodness so that others can see,
and help me to see your beauty in other people.

Amen.

Listening

O Holy Night
Stars (Skillet)

Day 24 – Weird Gifts

The Bible Bit

Matthew 2:11

They came to the house where the child was and saw him with his mother, Mary, and they bowed down and worshipped him. They opened their gifts and gave him treasures of gold, frankincense, and myrrh.

Stable Scene

Add Mary and Joseph.

In The Action

What unexpected visitors! I wonder what Mary and Joseph thought when three wise men knocked on their door. "Where will they park their camels? What can we offer them for food? I hope they booked a hotel because we certainly don't have room for them here!"

And what strange gifts!

"Errrm, OK. Thanks and all that, but what are we supposed to do with these?"

"Gold is nice, but we can't eat it. I could sell it, I suppose, but I'd probably get accused of stealing. I mean, why would a carpenter have a lump of gold? That's for a king, really."

"The incense is more use; we could use it to cover the smell of the nappies! But no, you're right. It's too special for that. This is the kind of incense that we burn to honour God."

"And myrrh? Oil for putting on for dead people? That's plain weird. Oh well, I guess they gave what they had."

To Think About

What do you have that you could give?

Responding

Dear God,

the wise men brought strange gifts to Jesus,
but that was OK with you.
I don't know if I have anything good enough to give,
but thank you that what I bring is OK with you.

Amen.

Listening

We Three Kings
Little Drummer Boy (For King and Country)

Day 25 – A Child Is Born

The Bible Bit

Isaiah 9:6

A child has been born to us; God has given a son to us.
He will be responsible for leading the people.
His name will be Wonderful Counsellor, Powerful God, Father Who Lives Forever, Prince of Peace.

Stable Scene

Add Jesus overnight, to be found on Christmas morning.

In The Action

Overnight, something changed. We did not see it happen. We did not hear it. But perhaps we felt it. Something changed.

Jesus is here. Jesus who came as a baby then grew to be a man. He has been here all through this journey, even when we could not see him. Immanuel, God-who-is-with-us.

So what do we do, now the story has finished? It's Christmas Day, and everyone has arrived in Bethlehem. I suppose they all go back. The wise men return to their country. The shepherds go back to their flocks. Mary and Joseph take Jesus home to Nazareth. But it's not the same.

The wise men go home, but they have knelt before the King of Kings. The shepherds go back to work, but they have met the Prince of Peace; they have heard angels sing of Good News for all people. Reaching Bethlehem was not the end of their journey. It was the start of a whole new adventure. The story has not finished, it has only just begun!

To Think About

Where are you on your journey?

Responding

Dear God,

thank you for Jesus.
Thank you for sending him to live with us that first Christmas.
Thank you that he lived and died and lived again to allow us to be your children.
Thank you for Christmas.

Amen.

Listening

Saviour's Day (Cliff Richard)   Hallelujah Chorus (Messiah)
O Come All Ye Faithful   What Child is This? (Greensleeves

Making Family Traditions

This book started life as a set of mini-booklets that I made for my children when they were very young. We still use them, and they've become a precious family tradition. We read one each day of Advent then hang it on the Christmas tree.

Here are ideas and instructions for making your family traditions using the photocopiable resources and simple household materials.

Scrolls – you can make paper scrolls from the daily readings and hang them on your Christmas tree each day.

Paper Chains – a fun way to count down to Christmas is to make the readings into paper chains. You can either add one link to the chain each day until you have the full chain, or you can make the full chain in advance and take one link off each day.

Posada Road – Posada is an Advent custom where figures of Mary and Joseph move from house to house during Advent, arriving at church on Christmas Eve. You can do your own Posada by making a simple road and moving Mary and Joseph a few steps along each day, arriving at Bethlehem on Christmas Eve.

Advent Labyrinth – if you don't have space for a road, you can coil the journey round into a labyrinth. A labyrinth is not a puzzle, but a single path that winds around to the centre.

Labyrinths have a long history in Christian prayer and meditation and are often used as mini-pilgrimages. You can stop and pray at each turn, or at the numbered places along the path. A labyrinth helps you to think about how you are travelling, as well as the destination.

You can make a table-sized labyrinth with the crib scene in the middle and move Mary and Joseph one stop along the journey each day. Alternatively, you can print out a smaller labyrinth and colour a section each day. This is an ideal mindfulness activity that can keep your hands occupied while you spend time with God.

Photocopiable Resources

This section contains sheets that you may reproduce. See copyright page for details.

Readings

The daily readings, numbered, and printed in a festive typeface. They are deliberately assorted so that you can copy each page onto different paper and have a colourful assortment.

Labyrinths

Five original labyrinth designs for use as templates to make large Advent labyrinths for your nativity crib figures, or for colouring.

Colouring Sheets

Nine extra colouring pages and blank templates for your own designs.

Instructions and Lists

After the photocopiable resources, there are instructions for the scrolls and paper chains, and for making a Posada Road or large floor labyrinth in a range of sizes.

Finally, there are lists of all the characters featured in the Stable Scene, with the order in which they are added or moved, and the daily readings with references.

1 God sent the angel Gabriel to Nazareth, a town in Galilee, to a virgin. She was engaged to marry a man named Joseph from the family of David. Her name was Mary. Luke 1:26-27

6 "I Mary said, "I am the servant of the Lord. Let this happen to me as you say!"

Then the angel went away.
Luke 1:38

11 "S The angel said, "She will give birth to a son, and you will name him Jesus, because he will save his people from their sins".
Matthew 1:21

16 An That night, some shepherds were in the fields nearby watching their sheep. Then an angel of the Lord stood before them. The glory of the Lord was shining around them, and they became very frightened. Luke 2:8-9

21 So the shepherds went quickly and found Mary and Joseph and the baby, who was lying in a feeding trough. When they had seen him, they told what the angels had said about this child. But Mary treasured these things and continued to think about them. Luke

2

The angel came to her and said, "Greetings! The Lord has blessed you and is with you." But Mary was very startled by what the angel said and wondered what this greeting might mean.   Luke 1:28-29

7

Then Mary said, "My soul praises the Lord; my heart rejoices in God my Saviour. From now on, all people will say that I am blessed, because the Powerful One has done great things for me. His name is holy."   Luke 1:46-49

12

All this happened to bring about what the Lord had said through the prophet: "The virgin will be pregnant. She will have a son, and they will name him Immanuel," which means "God is with us."   Matthew 1:22-23

17

The angel said to them, "Do not be afraid. I am bringing you good news that will be a great joy to all the people. Today your Saviour was born in the town of David. He is Christ, the Lord."   Luke 2:10-11

22

When Jesus was born, some wise men from the east came to Jerusalem. They asked, "Where is the baby who was born to be the king of the Jews? We saw his star in the east and have come to worship him."   Matthew 2:1-2

3

The angel said to her, "Don't be afraid, Mary; God has shown you his grace. Listen! You will become pregnant and give birth to a son, and you will name him Jesus."   Luke 1:30-31

8

M Mary was engaged to marry Joseph, but before they married, she learned she was pregnant by the power of the Holy Spirit.

Matthew 1:18

13

Augustus Caesar sent an order that all people must list their names in a register. So Joseph left Nazareth and went to Bethlehem in Judea, known as the town of David. Joseph registered with Mary, to whom he was engaged and who was now pregnant.

Luke 2:1-5

18

The angel said, "This is how you will know him: You will find a baby wrapped in pieces of cloth and lying in a feeding box."

Luke 2:12

23

Herod sent the wise men to Bethlehem. The star that they had seen in the east went before them until it stopped above the place where the child was. When

4 "He will be great and will be called the Son of the Most High. The Lord God will give him the throne of King David, his ancestor. He will rule over the people of Jacob forever, and his kingdom will never end." Luke 1:32-33

9 Because Mary's husband, Joseph, was a good man, he did not want to disgrace her in public, so he planned to divorce her secretly. Matthew 1:19

14 While they were in Bethlehem, the time came for Mary to have the baby, and she gave birth to her first son. Because there were no rooms left in the inn, she wrapped the baby with pieces of cloth and laid him in a feeding trough. Luke 2:6-7

19 Then a very large group of angels from heaven joined the first angel, praising God and saying: "Give glory to God in heaven, and on earth let there be peace among the people who please God." Luke 2:13-14

24 They came to the house where the child was and saw him with his mother, Mary, and they bowed down and worshiped him. They opened their gifts and gave him treasures of gold, frankincense, and myrrh. Matthew 2:11

5 Mary said to the angel, "How will this happen since I am a virgin?" The angel said to Mary, "The Holy Spirit will come upon you, and the power of the Most High will cover you. For this reason the baby will be holy and will be called the Son of God."   Luke 1:34-35

10 An angel of the Lord came to Joseph in a dream. The angel said, "Joseph, descendant of David, don't be afraid to take Mary as your wife, because the baby in her is from the Holy Spirit."   Matthew 1:20

15 The Word became a human and lived among us. We saw his glory – the glory that belongs to the only Son of the Father – and he was full of grace and truth.   John 1:14

20 The prophet wrote about this in the Scriptures: "But you, Bethlehem, in the land of Judah, are not just an insignificant village in Judah. A ruler will come from you who will be like a shepherd for my people Israel."   Matthew 2:5-6

25 A child has been born to us; God has given a son to us. He will be responsible for leading the people. His name will be Wonderful Counsellor,

Walking to Bethlehem
An Advent Journey

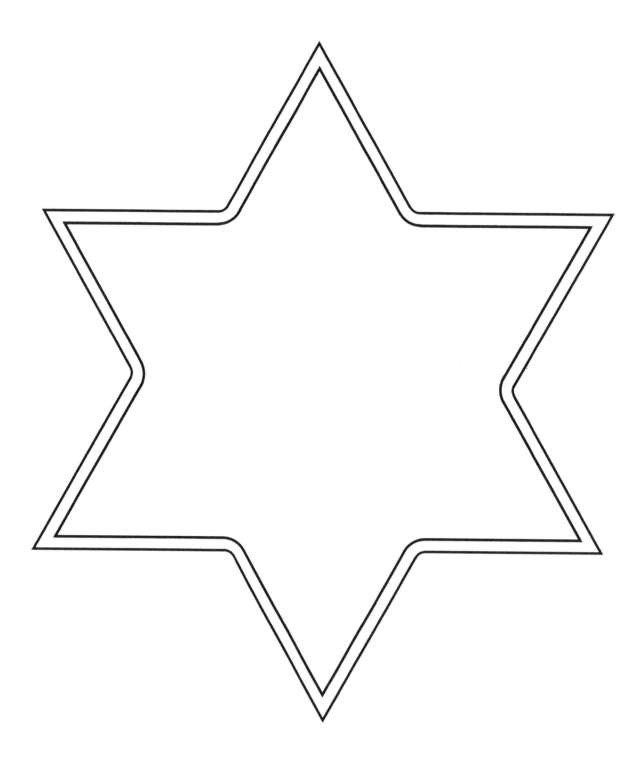

Instructions and Lists

Scrolls

You will need:

- 25 daily readings printed onto white or coloured paper
- Teabag
- Ribbon or yarn for hanging

What to do:

1. Print out the readings onto white or coloured paper. Do not trim the edges.
2. Dip a finger in some water and draw wet lines around the readings. Let the paper soak for a minute, then carefully tear the readings apart down the wet lines, giving ragged edges.
3. Soak a tea bag in water and use it to 'age' the paper. You can either dab the tea bag all over the paper (this looks best on white) or dab only the torn edges.
4. Roll the paper strips up, starting from the not-number end, and leave them to dry.
5. Add hanging loops to the corners near the number (punch a hole or attach with tape) and store your scrolls in a box, ready to hang on the tree each day.

Paper Chains

You will need:

- 25 daily readings printed onto coloured paper
- Scissors (possibly wavy ones)
- Coloured pens or highlighters
- Glue stick

What to do:

1. Cut the readings into long strips, with straight or wavy edges.
2. Use pens to decorate the strips. Highlighted edges look good.
3. Glue each strip into a loop, threading each loop through the one from the day before to make a chain.

You have two options with a paper chain: as a count-down calendar, or a count-up.

To count up to Christmas, have the strips in a pile and add one to the chain each day until you have the whole story chain on Christmas Day.

For a count-down calendar, make the whole chain in advance and carefully cut one strip from the chain each day. When you have read it, you could roll it into a scroll to hang on the tree if you like.

Posada Road

You can follow Mary and Joseph's journey to Bethlehem by making Posada Road. It is a great visual marker of the long wait for Christmas, and children love moving the figures each day. If you build your crib at the end of the road, you can watch Mary and Joseph get closer each day, arriving at Bethlehem on Christmas Eve.

You will need:

- Coarse sandpaper
- Stapler
- Green or brown paint
- PVA glue
- Moss or green yarn clippings
- Wooden or felt numbers 1 to 24, or permanent marker pen

Choose how long and wide you want your road to be. It should be at least 20 times as long as it is wide. You could place it along a table or mantlepiece, along a hallway or even up the stairs!

Here are some dimensions in cm for standard sandpaper of 23 x 28cm (9 x 11"):

Number of sheets	Cut each sheet into	Each piece	Path length	Path width	Mary and Joseph move each day
1	5	5 x 28	130	5	5
2	4	6 x 28	200	6	8
3	3	8 x 28	240	8	10
4	3	8 x 28	320	8	13
5	2	12 x 28	270	12	11
6	2	12 x 28	320	12	13
7	2	12 x 28	370	12	15

What to do:

1. Cut the sandpaper sheets into long strips and join them with staples.
2. Mix the green / brown paint with PVA glue and dab it thickly along the sides of the road.
3. Scatter moss or yarn clippings in the wet paint to give it texture.
4. Glue the numbers 1 to 24 evenly along the path, or mark the numbers with a pen.
5. Place the road so that it ends at the crib. Mary and Joseph get to the end of the road on Christmas Eve.
6. If you like, you can place the other figures along the road on the appropriate days. (See The Stable Scene for a list of characters and days.) You can add the figures to the crib as Mary and Joseph meet them on the road.

Advent Labyrinth

A labyrinth is like a road, but coiled up to take less room. You can use the photocopiable pages for a small, colour-in labyrinth. There are several designs to choose from, and you can add your own decorations.

Alternatively, make a table-sized labyrinth and use the Mary and Joseph characters from your Stable Scene to walk through it.

If you have room, you can build the crib in the middle so that Mary and Joseph arrive there on Christmas Eve.

Here are instructions for making a table-sized labyrinth for an Advent centrepiece.

You Will Need:

- Fabric, felt, wood or carpet off-cut
- Pencil or washable marker
- Paints or marker pens
- Ruler
- String
- Wooden or felt numbers 1 to 24 (optional)

Choose how wide you want your finished labyrinth to be, and how wide you want the centre and paths. Here are some suggested dimensions, in cm:

Outside diameter	Path width	Centre diameter	Circle radii							
40	2	12	6	8	10	12	14	16	18	20
60	3	18	9	12	15	18	21	24	27	30
80	4	24	12	16	20	24	28	32	36	40
100	5	30	15	20	25	30	35	40	45	50

For example, if you want a finished size of 100cm with a 30cm circle in the middle for your crib scene, you need to draw circles with radii of 15cm, 20cm, 25cm, and so on until the largest has a radius of 50cm.

This design is based on a full-sized grass labyrinth in Launde Abbey, Leicestershire, England.

You can use the same principle for making other designs, adjusting the number of paths to suit.

What To Do:

1. Use the pencil and string to lightly mark the largest circle (as shown in the diagram) on your material. Do not make the pencil lines too dark because you will only need parts of them.

2. Cut out the circle and neaten the edges if necessary.

3. Lightly mark the other circles, making sure they have the same centre.

4. Lightly mark lines from the centre to the edge at the quarters: top, bottom, right and left (as shown in the diagram). The line at the bottom marks the entrance.

5. Add one vertical line to the left of the line for the entrance, and one to the right (as shown in the diagram). These make the paths for the way in and the way to the centre. The paths should be the same width as the gaps between your circles. (See table above for path widths.)

6. Following the pattern, erase parts of the circles and lines, making all gaps the same width as the gap between your circles. It should look like the grey lines in the diagram.

7. When you are sure you have the lines right, go over them in permanent marker or paint.

8. If you are using fabric or felt, you can sew over the lines with knitting wools.

9. Add 'blobs' to the ends of lines or any other decorative features as required.

10. Add date markers in pen or paint, or by glueing felt or wooden numbers in place.

Making The Stable Scene

This is a wonderful way to watch the build up to Christmas. Each day you add a character or an item to your crib or move the wise men closer on their long journey. (The wise men need four places to stay, the last of which should be close to the crib.)

This scene building works beautifully in conjunction with a Posada Road or a large labyrinth, but can be used separately, too.

Characters

Mary	
Joseph	
Jesus	
Wise Men (3)	Balthazar, Melchior, Gaspar
Angels (5)	Gabriel, Michael, Uriel, Zadkiel, Raphael
Shepherds (2)	Laban, Amos
Animals (6)	1 donkey, 2 sheep, 3 other farm animals
Things (3)	stable, manger, star

Mary, Joseph and Gabriel are named in the story. The wise men and other angels have traditional names. Laban and Amon are Old Testament shepherds. Feel free to use the names or not.

Building the Scene

Day 1	Add Gabriel (angel)		Day 13	Add donkey
Day 2	Place Balthazar (wise man) far off		Day 14	Add manger
Day 3	Place Melchior (wise man) far off		Day 15	Move wise men closer
Day 4	Place Gaspar (wise man) far off		Day 16	Add Michael (angel)
Day 5	Add stable		Day 17	Add Uriel (angel)
Day 6	Add sheep		Day 18	Add Zadkiel (angel)
Day 7	Add star		Day 19	Add Raphael (angel)
Day 8	Add sheep		Day 20	Add Laban (shepherd)
Day 9	Move wise men closer		Day 21	Add Amos (shepherd)
Day 10	Add animal		Day 22	Move wise men closer
Day 11	Add animal		Day 23	Add wise men
Day 12	Add animal		Day 24	Add Mary and Joseph
			Day 25	Add Jesus overnight

The Bible Bits

These are the Bible texts that are used for the 25 readings. You can turn the readings into paper chains or scrolls to hang on your tree if you like (see instructions earlier).

Day 1	Luke 1:26-27	God sent the angel Gabriel …
Day 2	Luke 1:28-29	"Greetings! The Lord has blessed you …
Day 3	Luke 1:30-31	The angel said to her, "Don't be afraid, Mary …
Day 4	Luke 1:32-33	"He will be great …
Day 5	Luke 1:34-35	"How will this happen …
Day 6	Luke 1:38	"I am the servant of the Lord …
Day 7	Luke 1:46-49	And Mary said: "My soul praises the Lord …
Day 8	Matthew 1:18	Mary was engaged to marry Joseph …
Day 9	Matthew 1:19	… he had in mind to divorce her secretly.
Day 10	Matthew 1:20	"Don't be afraid to take Mary as your wife …
Day 11	Matthew 1:21	"You will name him Jesus …
Day 12	Matthew 1:22-23	… Immanuel," which means "God is with us".
Day 13	Luke 2:1, 4-5	Augustus Caesar sent an order …
Day 14	Luke 2:6-7	The time came for Mary to have the baby …
Day 15	John 1:14	The Word became a human …
Day 16	Luke 2:8-9	Some shepherds were in the fields nearby …
Day 17	Luke 2:10-11	The angel said to them, "Do not be afraid …
Day 18	Luke 2:12	"This is how you will know him …
Day 19	Luke 2:13-14	"Give glory to God in heaven …
Day 20	Matthew 2:5-6	But you, Bethlehem, in the land of Judah …
Day 21	Luke 2:16-17, 19	So the shepherds went quickly …
Day 22	Matthew 2:1-2	Wise men from the east …
Day 23	Matthew 2:8-10	The star that they had seen in the east …
Day 24	Matthew 2:11	… gold, frankincense and myrrh.
Day 25	Isaiah 9:6	A child has been born to us …

About the Author

Hi, I'm Fay.

Here I am, signing a book in one of my favourite places, the library of my college in Cambridge. (I'm not writing in a library book, honest.)

In alphabetical order, I am an author, blogger, geek, knitologist, mathematician, mum, tea-bibber, teacher, theology researcher and Trekkie.

I'm a member of the all-age worship and Messy Church teams at my large, lively, Anglican church, and I play the guitar (badly) for our women's group.

I have solo-authored six books in addition to this one, several of which have topped their respective charts on Amazon. I am a contributory author to four more books, some indie-published, some traditional. I also write a popular weekly blog, The Reflectionary, and have published papers in academic journals.

When not writing, I teach maths for a living and spend most of the rest of the time being creative. I live with my children and pet dragon in the English Midlands in a house full of glue sticks and mess (which I blame on the kids, but really, it's me).

Contact

If you have any questions, comments or feedback, I'd love to hear from you. No, really, I would. After all, you, dear reader, are the very reason I write. Without you it would be like the UK's Eurovision entry ... pointless.

You can drop me a line (fay@fayrowland.co.uk) and let me know how your Advent is going. May you have a joyful and peaceful Christmas.

blessings,

Other Publications

A Bucketful of Ideas for Church Drama

"Parables as Jesus would have told them – witty and thought-provoking."

"Thirty Pieces of Chocolate is a fine pun-run."

#1 Best-Seller in Puppet

A(nother) Bucketful of Ideas for Church Drama

14 scripts including CRISP-tingle, a pop-up nativity, and lots more.

"Delivers the timeless truths of scripture in a modern and punchy manner."

God Is With Us – Everywhere!

Featuring a cool Gabriel, terrified shepherds and three confused scientists, this witty yet poignant Nativity is perfect for your school or church production.

"Thank you for your script, we had it at our online carol service yesterday - and it went down a storm!"

#1 Best-Seller in Christian Youth Ministry!

Walking to Bethlehem

25 imaginative devotions for adults and children, with reflective colouring and craft ideas.

"Travel from BC to AD to focus your mind on the road to Bethlehem. Fun and devotional, practical and creative."

#1 Best-Seller in Advent

The Big Story

Discover the Bible as one big story of God and God's people, from the very beginning of everything up to the wonder of Easter.

#1 Best-Seller in Bible

Perfect for personal devotions, for weekly Bible studies and youth groups, discover The Big Story today.

Broken Bits & Weirdness

Meet nine of the Bible's dismal failures and learn how God still loves them (and us), even with our Broken Bits & Weirdness.

With Bible notes, crafts, cooking, colouring and other resources, and studies for Good Friday and Easter Day, this is perfect for Lent or any time of year.

#1 Best-Seller in Bible

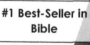

So You've Finished Writing. Now What?

You've finished the writing – brilliant! Well done.

Now you have to get your words out there, into the sweaty mitts* of your readers. But how?

Best-selling non-fiction author, Fay guides you with humour and helpful insight through the maze of the editing process and out into the wonderful world of publishing.

Whether you write books, articles, poems or self-help guides to frog wrestling, there are ways for you to get your words out there.

So what are you waiting for, the credits?

Perfect for new authors, aspiring authors and anyone who has ever pressed 'send' and then spotted the typo. Which is all of us.

* Eeew!

Creativity Matters

Join thirteen authors as they share their passion for why you should write in their genre and find your own passion as you read.

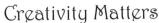

In my chapter, 'Why Write Drama?', you can discover what makes drama sparkle, and why you shouldn't take your gran to see a Greek satyr play!

URC Prayer Handbooks

I have been a commissioned author for the URC's prayer handbooks for several years.

They are full of original, passionate, quirky, and relevant prayers, this year focussing on a theme of 'Freed to Live!'

Each Sunday has several prayers linked to readings from the Revised Common Lectionary. The prayers are suitable for both congregational and private use, using contemporary language and covering a broad range of topics.

You can buy the most recent prayer handbooks at the URC's website shop.

Credits

Cover illustration by Elizabeth Thomas

Other images by the author or public domain.

All Bible texts quoted are from the New Century Version.

New Century Version®. Copyright © 2005 by Thomas Nelson. Used by permission. All rights reserved.

Pronouns have been changed to indicate person where required for clarity, and punctuation and spelling amended as needed. Some passages have been abridged.

Some of this material has previously appeared in The Reflectionary, a weekly blog of resources for interactive worship. You can follow The Reflectionary on Facebook (search for Reflectionary) or join our mailing list by visiting www.reflectionary.org.

If you like this book, visit www.fayrowland.co.uk to see other publications by the same author.

Made in the USA
Coppell, TX
02 December 2021